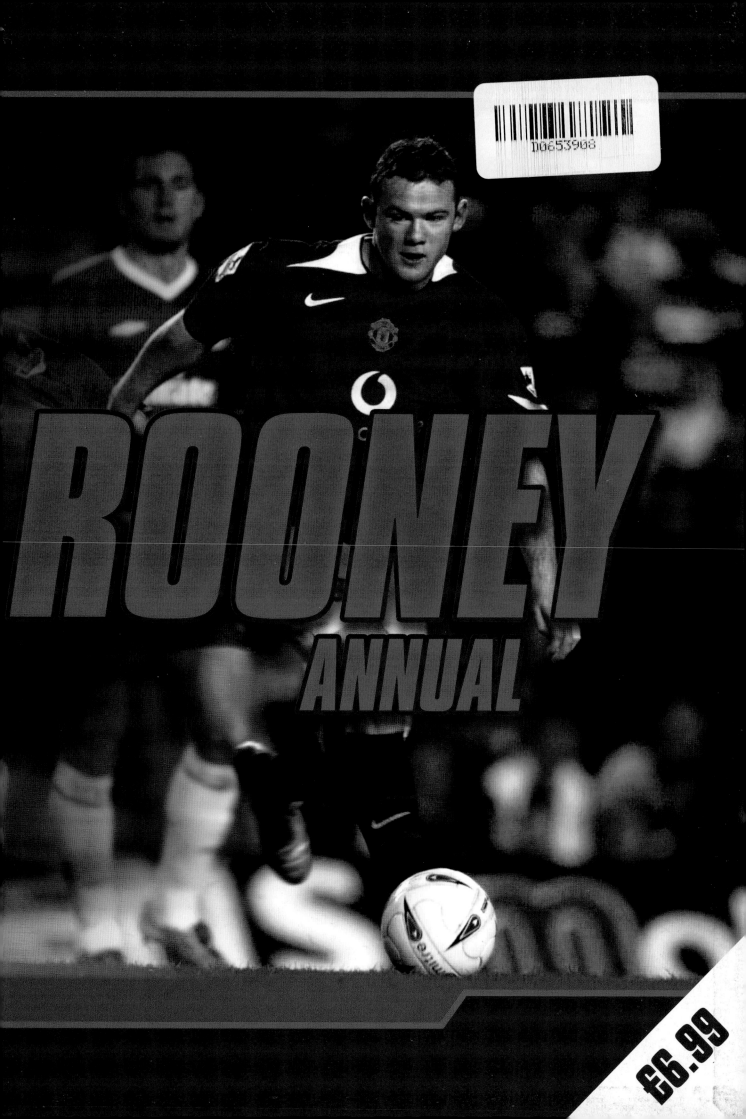

ROONEY
ANNUAL

£6.99

WAYNE ROONEY
WAYNE ROONEY
WAYNE ROONEY
WAYNE ROONEY

WAYNE ROONEY ANNUAL

CONTENTS

WAYNE ROONEY
WAYNE ROONEY
WAYNE ROONEY
WAYNE ROONEY

UNOFFICIAL

WAYNE ROONEY
WONDER KID

After watching 16-year-old Wayne Rooney score his famous wonder-goal against Arsenal in October 2002, the Gunners' boss Arsene Wenger said: 'He is the most complete young English footballer I have seen since I've been in the country.'

That's high praise indeed, especially as Mr Wenger has worked with some of the world's finest footballing talents at both club level and international level.

Since that memorable day young Wayne has risen rapidly to the very heights of English football. And this book tells the story of his fabulous career so far: his amazing record in youth team football, his exciting times with two of England's top clubs and his rise to international superstardom.

WE HOPE YOU ENJOY READING THE **WAYNE ROONEY ANNUAL...**

ROONEY
AT A GLANCE

Full Name:	Wayne Mark Rooney
Birthdate:	24 October 1985
Birthplace:	Croxteth, Liverpool
Starsign:	Scorpio
Height:	5' 10"
Weight:	12st 4lb (variable)
Mum:	Jeanette
Dad:	Wayne
Brothers:	Graham & John
Fiancé:	Colleen

ONCE IN A BLUE MOON

Wayne Mark Rooney, the boy destined to become one of the biggest stars in English soccer, entered the world on 24 October 1985, in the Liverpool suburb of Croxteth. The house he was bought up in stands within striking distance of Goodison Park, home of the famous Everton Football Club.

Blue was definitely the colour in the Rooney household when the lad was growing up. In fact, Wayne's father – also called Wayne – planted his firstborn son's Evertonian roots on the day the boy was born, buying him a replica of the Toffees' shirt as worn by the team in the 1985-86 campaign.

Wayne's dad had once enjoyed some time in the sporting spotlight as a promising amateur boxer; his mum, Jeanette Rooney, was a school-dinner lady. Wayne Jnr is the eldest of three brothers and, like him, young Graham and John both grew up as fervent Everton supporters.

In the previous season – 1984-85 – Everton had become Champions of England for the eighth time in their history. That title win broke the seeming monopoly of city neighbours Liverpool who had won the League three times in succession before the Toffees' topped the table at the end of that season.

The 1984-85 campaign also brought Everton's only European success to date. Having won the

1984 FA Cup final with a 2-0 victory over Watford at Wembley, the Toffees had progressed to beat Rapid Vienna 3-1 in the 1985 European Cup-Winners' Cup final in Rotterdam just five months before Wayne Rooney was born.

For Wayne Rooney Snr and everyone else in Merseyside's blue zone, Everton's success was made even sweeter because they had finished with a brilliant margin of no less than 13 points ahead of the Anfield Reds. And the icing on Everton's cake that season came with two 1-0 victories over Liverpool.

The Toffees were still going strong at the time of little Wayne's birth, a third of the way through the 1985-86 campaign. That was the season in which England's superstar striker Gary Lineker played for Everton alongside such legendary Blues as Peter Reid, Graeme Sharp, Paul Bracewell and Neville Southall. This time the Toffees would finish runners-up in the League table to – you've guessed it – Liverpool!

The two Merseyside giants also met in the 1986 FA Cup final at Wembley. Gary Lineker scored the opening goal that day, only to see his side eventually lose 3-1 as Liverpool wrapped up the elusive 'double'.

And so it was in an atmosphere of intense blue/red rivalry that the young Wayne Rooney grew up...

WAYNE ROONEY
WAYNE ROONEY
WAYNE ROONEY
WAYNE ROONEY

WAYNE IN EVERTON BLUE

ONCE IN A
BLUE MOON

It was soon obvious that the youngster was going to be quite a footballer when he grew up. From a very early age he would spend hours kicking a ball around. He couldn't know it then of course, but he was already developing the skills that would take him to the very top of the game.

Like his father and brother Graham, Wayne also boxed for a while, and by all accounts he was quite a talented fighter with a pretty hefty punch. But football was always his passion and he grabbed every opportunity to play the game he loved. He was always a star player at school, both in the playground and in organised games.

All agreed that he possessed the power, the strength and, more importantly, the natural talent to one day become a professional footballer.

When Everton crossed Stanley Park to play Liverpool at Anfield in the Merseyside derby on 20 November 1996, 11-year-old Wayne was the Toffees' mascot for the day. In the company of skipper Dave Watson he strode onto the Anfield turf ahead of the rest of the blue-clad team which also included the likes of super-keeper Neville Southall, flying Russian winger Andrei Kanchelskis, Welsh international Gary Speed and England star Nick Barmby. It was a very proud moment for the Everton-mad lad. The

IF EVERTON HADN'T MADE THEIR MOVE WHEN THEY DID, THE UNTHINKABLE MIGHT HAVE HAPPENED — WAYNE ROONEY COULD HAVE BECOME A MERSEYSIDE RED!

As a junior he went to Our Lady & St Swithins School and played for Liverpool Schools Under-11s, scoring 99 goals for them in a single season. He also played for other teams outside school hours. They included Western Approaches, Copplehouse, East Villa and Pye FC – it was as a Pye-boy that Wayne won a Golden Boot award as top-scorer in a tournament organised by British Telecom.

Wayne moved up to the De La Salle Comprehensive and helped their team attain a league and cup 'double' in his first year there. As time went by everyone – schoolmates and teachers alike – recognised Wayne's special talents on the football pitch. It is said that certain sports-mad teachers used to make a point of watching him in action with a ball at his feet during the inevitable break-time kick-around.

game ended in a 1-1 draw: Robbie Fowler firing the Reds ahead on 30 minutes and Gary Speed grabbing a late equaliser for the Blues. By that time the Goodison Park club had taken note of the talented young Rooney and in football's time-honoured tradition they had invited him to train with other promising juniors at their Bellefields coaching complex.

Luckily, the club had made its move in the nick of time – rivals Liverpool were actually quickest off the mark in inviting Wayne to attend their Melwood headquarters. Obviously, as a wannabe professional player, the youngster could hardly refuse Liverpool's approach so he went along to Melwood for a trial (in his favourite Everton shirt!). The Everton approach came along soon afterwards and he accepted like a shot.

ONCE IN A BLUE MOON

And so, shortly before his tenth birthday, Wayne Rooney had made the first step on the ladder to professional status when he enrolled at the Everton Academy. From that point onwards, the future superstar rose rapidly through the Blue ranks, often playing in teams of an older age limit as he had done at school. He was only 13 when selected for the Under-15s. Two years later he was in the Toffees' Under-17s side, as a 15-year-old.

International recognition came in November 2000 with Wayne's selection for England's Under-15s in the Victory Shield against Wales, which ended in a 1-1 draw. In his next Under-15 appearance he netted the opening goal in a 5-0 win against Scotland. He also played in a 1-1 draw with Spain in February 2001 and scored the first goal in a 3-0 win against Canada two months later.

By then he had already turned out for Everton's Under-19s. In one match against Liverpool's Youth team he came on as a late sub when the Reds were leading 2-1 – and made all the difference, scoring twice in the last 15 minutes to earn the Blues a great victory. With performances like these there were those who felt he was good enough to be playing in Everton's first-team even before he was eligible to do so!

It was the 2001-02 FA Youth Cup that would really spread the name of Wayne Rooney around the country. His inspired performances in the competition helped the Blues into the final. He scored both goals in the 2-0 win against West Brom in the Fourth Round, then repeated the feat against Manchester City in Round Five as Everton won 4-2. In the quarter-final he scored again and created Everton's second goal as they came back from a one-goal deficit to beat Nottingham Forest 2-1.

Wayne topped all of that with a stunning performance and two goals – one of them quite magical in the semi-final second-leg against Spurs

at White Hart Lane, helping Everton to progress with a 4-2 aggregate victory. After the second game Spurs' boss Glenn Hoddle asked about the likelihood of young Rooney's future availability on the transfer market, only to be told that the lad was not for sale at any price. Hoddle's enquiry was just one among many to come from equally envious managers at other clubs over the coming months. Aston Villa provided Everton's opposition in the two-legged FA Youth Cup final, having eliminated Wimbledon, Tranmere Rovers, Brighton, Fulham and Barnsley along the way to the last stage.

A crowd of more than 15,000 turned out to see the young Blues in action in the first-leg at Goodison Park on 14 May 2002, and were rewarded with a stunning performance from Wonder Kid Wayne. He scored the first goal, on 25 minutes, and was a constant presence throughout the match, urging, cajoling and creating openings and chances for his team-mates. Unfortunately for Everton, Villa's lads were on fire and two goals from Stefan Moore, one from Luke Moore and another from Peter Hynes all contributed to a thoroughly convincing 4-1 victory for the away side.

Four days later Everton's boys had it all to do again in the second-leg at Villa Park. It was asking a lot, even with Wayne Rooney in the side. In the event Villa did themselves proud by protecting their overall lead even though Everton took the game 1-0 through Scott Brown's 75th minute goal. Wayne was the star of the show making more than half a dozen goal attempts and earning the Player of the Final award.

By then Wayne was well established as a member of England's Under-17 team, having played a handful of games and scoring single goals against Lithuania and Yugoslavia, plus a stunning hat-tick in a 4-1 win against Spain's Under-17s just four days before the first-leg of the FA Youth Cup final.

Nine months later he would break into England's senior set-up.

WAYNE ROONEY
WAYNE ROONEY
WAYNE ROONEY
WAYNE ROONEY

WHAT'S SO SPECIAL ABOUT WAYNE ROONEY?

HMM. LET'S SEE? HERE ARE HALF A DOZEN REASONS WHY WAYNE IS CONSIDERED THE BEST OF THE LOT...

1. HE READS THE GAME TO PERFECTION...
Wayne has an instinctive footballing brain. Like all the great players of the past he is constantly aware of everything that's going on around him. This gives him a fine positional sense and makes his distribution of the ball extremely effective.

2. HE IS BRIMFUL OF CONFIDENCE...
Wayne shares another indispensable quality with the game's true greats – sheer confidence. He knows what he wants to do with the ball. And he knows exactly how to do it.

3. HE HAS GREAT SKILL...
Wayne is a natural ball-player with a whole repertoire of tricks, twists and turns that can baffle any opponent into submission.

4. HE HAS GREAT PACE...
Whenever necessary, young Rooney can put on a spurt of speed to match anyone in the Premier League.

5. HE IS A DEADLY FINISHER...
Whether smashing the ball into the net from 30-yards, subtly stroking it across the line from close range or delicately chipping a helpless 'keeper, Wayne rarely misses when an opportunity to score presents itself.

6. HE HAS GREAT STRENGTH...
The lad is as tough as old boots – the last thing an opponent wants to see is Wayne Rooney running at them with the ball at his feet, or to see him lining-up for a tackle.

PUT ALL THAT TOGETHER AND YOU GET THE ROONEY EFFECT!

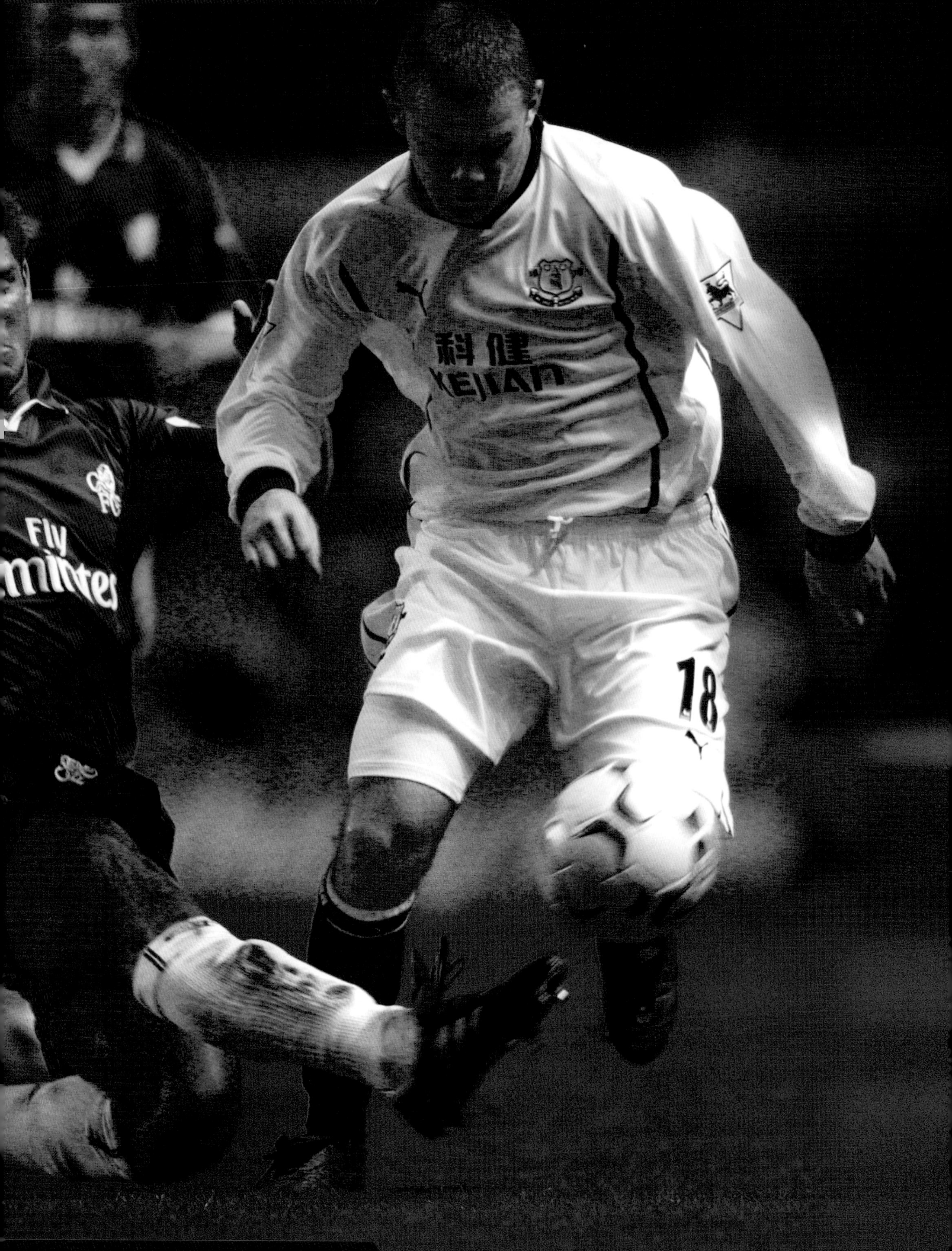
科健
KEJIAN
18
Fly
Emirates

WAYNE ROONEY
WAYNE ROONEY
WAYNE ROONEY
WAYNE ROONEY

GOOD TIMES AT

GOODISON

Along with all the other Everton Academy lads, Wayne had watched anxiously throughout the 2001-02 season as the club's senior side endured a frustrating mid-table battle in the Premiership, finally finishing in 15th place.

To make matters worse, Middlesbrough eliminated them in the quarter-finals of the FA Cup while in the League Cup they lost on penalties to Crystal Palace as early as the Second Round. Everton had been managed since 1998 by former Glasgow Rangers boss Walter Smith, but had never finished higher than 14th in the Premiership during his time in charge. In March 2002, he was replaced in the Goodison Park hot-seat by another Scotsman, David Moyes, who was about to become a hugely influential figure in the development of football's hottest young property.

Moyes had led Preston to the Second Division championship in 1999-2000 and was an old hand at the business of nurturing young footballers. In 1995, for instance, he had taken the emerging David Beckham under his wing when the Manchester United starlet spent a brief loan spell in which he made his football League debut with the Deepdale club.

As Alex Ferguson had once done with the likes of Ryan Giggs and Beckham in their early days at Old Trafford, the new Everton manager was determined to shield his latest protégé, Wayne Rooney, from the glare of the media spotlight. The sporting pages had already dubbed the youngster a 'Teenage Sensation' as he continued to impress on Everton's pre-season tour of Scotland in the summer of 2002.

Just before the start of the 2002-03 campaign Wayne made his first senior appearance at Goodison Park in a friendly against Spanish giants Atletico Bilbao. So, the promising 16-year-old knew he was in with at least a chance of taking part in Everton's opening game of their 100th top-flight season.

Following the old footballing adage 'if he's good enough, he's old enough' David Moyes decided to throw Wayne in at the deep end by including him in the starting line-up for Everton's first Premiership match, against Spurs, at Goodison Park on 17 August 2002. His first-team selection at the tender age of 16 years and 298 days placed him second only to local hero Joe Royle as the Toffees' youngest-ever debutant.

Young Rooney displayed bags of confidence and didn't seem at all phased by the occasion. He even helped to create Everton's opening goal, supplying the telling pass from which Mark Pembridge scored. Rooney was removed from the action and substituted by Niclaus Alexandersson in the 77th minute, but by then the Everton faithful were further convinced that all those rumours were true – the new kid on the Goodison block really was something special. The game ended in a 2-2 draw.

GOOD TIMES AT
GOODISON

Seven days later Wayne came on as a sub for Alexandersson in the 74th minute of Everton's 1-0 win at Sunderland's magnificent Stadium of Light. He then played throughout the home game against Birmingham. Everton's Alan Stubbs was sent off just before half-time and it was left to David Unsworth to salvage a point with a dramatic last-minute equaliser.

Next came another substitute appearance for Wayne, in the 64th minute against Manchester City at Maine Road, when the Toffees were 2-1 down. The final score-line was 3-1 to City, with their latest signing Nicholas Anelka netting a stunning hat-trick.

Wayne followed that game with two more substitute appearances, in a 1-0 defeat at Southampton's St Mary's Stadium and a 2-1 win against Middlesbrough at Goodison Park with Kevin Campbell netting both Toffees' goals.

In their next Premiership fixture and despite a spirited fight-back, Everton lost 3-2 at Aston Villa. Early in the game Wayne clashed with Steve Staunton, leaving the defender with a cut above his eye. The young Evertonian was substituted by Alexandersson in the 77th minute and ended the game with the first yellow card of his senior career.

After sitting out the whole of Everton's next game, a 2-0 win against Fulham, Wayne again warmed the bench for the club's first cup-tie of 2002. It was a League Cup meeting with Third Division Wrexham at the Racecourse Ground on 1 October 2002, twenty-three days before his 17th birthday. Thanks to a first-half strike by Kevin Campbell, Everton were leading 1-0 when David Moyes sent Rooney on in the 63rd minute as a sub for the Canadian international Tomaz Radzinski.

ROONEY BRAKES TOMMY LAWTON'S 65 YEAR OLD RECORD TO BECOME EVERTON'S YOUNGEST EVER GOALSCORER.

The youngster immediately began turning on the magic and in the 82nd minute he netted his first senior goal for the club. It was a proud moment for the player and an historic one – he had just broken Tommy Lawton's 65-year-old record to become Everton's youngest-ever goalscorer. Seven minutes later Rooney scored again, stealing the show and ensuring the Toffees' an easy passage to the next stage of the competition.

If Everton's fans were delighted by what they'd seen that day, they didn't have to wait long for something extra-special from the boy Rooney. It didn't come in the next game, in which Wayne again replaced Radzinski, which was a 3-0 defeat at Manchester United. It came in the game after that.

GOOD TIMES AT
GOODISON

Reigning Premier League champions Arsenal arrived at Goodison Park on 19 October 2002 boasting a remarkable run of 30 League games without defeat. The Gunners took the lead on eight minutes through Freddie Ljungberg. But the Toffees fought back and Radzinski equalised 14 minutes later.

With ten minutes left to play, David Moyes once again sent Rooney on in place of Radzinski. The lad settled in well, displaying all his usual determination, confidence and verve, although as the game progressed it looked ever more likely that the points would be shared and Arsenal would extend that brilliant unbeaten run.

Injury time was approaching when the magic happened. Spotting Arsenal's 'keeper David Seaman slightly off his line, Wayne unleashed a sensational 30-yard drive that flew goal-wards, swerved a little in its trajectory and beat England's star goalie all ends up to make it 2-1 to Everton.

The Toffees had won a famous victory; the Gunners had suffered a rare defeat. And it was all thanks to the quick thinking, the raw power and the unquestionable talent of Wayne Rooney.

After the game Wayne could hardly hide his delight. 'When I got the ball I was only ever going to shoot,' he said. 'It was an unbelievable feeling seeing it hit the net. I'll never forget that goal.'

The strike was also another one for the record books. At 16 years, 360 days Wayne had become the Premier League's youngest-ever scorer.

WAYNE ROONEY
WAYNE ROONEY
WAYNE ROONEY
WAYNE ROONEY

EVERTON'S ROLL OF HONOUR

ENGLISH CHAMPIONS
1890-91, 1914-15, 1927-28, 1931-32, 1938-39, 1962-63, 1969-70, 1984-85, 1986-87 (9 times)

FA CUP WINNERS
1906, 1933, 1966, 1984, 1995 (five times)

EUROPEAN CUP-WINNERS CUP WINNERS
1984-85 (once)

The brilliant result against Arsenal proved to be the inspiration Everton needed to push for a higher than usual Premier League placing.

Throughout the remainder of the 2002-03 campaign, Wayne would take his tally to 14 full and 19 substitute appearances. He scored five more League goals, against Leeds (earning the Toffees their first League victory at Elland Road in 49 years), Blackburn, Arsenal (again), Newcastle and Aston Villa. This made him Everton's third top scorer of the season behind Radzinski (11) and Campbell (10), all of whom helped Everton to a 7th-place finish in the 2002-03 Premiership campaign, just missing out on a UEFA Cup placing.

The 'Teenage Sensation' also grabbed the headlines when he was named the BBC's Young Sports Personality of the Year for 2002 and again when he eventually signed a contract with Everton in January 2003. The deal reportedly made him an instant millionaire and assured him of a pay packet worth around £14,000 per week.

And he had now made the breakthrough at full international level...

ENGLAND CALLING!

W ayne had made only six Premiership starts in Everton's colours when England coach Sven-Goran Eriksson selected him for his squad to face Australia in a friendly encounter at West Ham's Upton Park ground.

The game, on 12 February 2003, was part of Sven's team-assessing exercise during the first phase of England's qualifying campaign for the 2004 European Championship finals in Portugal. Drawn in Group 7, along with Turkey, Slovakia, Macedonia and Liechtenstein, the Three Lions had played just two games in the campaign to date – recording a 2-1 victory in Slovakia and a disappointing 2-2 draw with Macedonia at Southampton's St Mary's Stadium.

In theory the game against Australia would give Sven and his backroom team the opportunity to experiment with his line-up. In the event he sent on two different teams, one in the first half, one in the second.

Wayne sat out the first half, during which the visiting Socceroos – utterly determined to do their best against the Three Lions built up a 2-0 lead. In the second period Sven sent him on and he enlivened England's attack, making one long-range attempt at goal, making a claim for a penalty and helping to create England's only goal, scored by Francis Jeffers.

Although England lost the match 3-1, the boy Rooney duly wrote his name in the history books. At just 17 years and 111 days of age he had become England's youngest-ever full international. Six weeks after his historical Three Lions debut, Wayne came on as a 79th minute sub for Emile Heskey when England beat European qualifying Group 7 contenders Liechtenstein in Vaduz on 29 March.

In what had been a pretty uninspired performance England were leading 2-0 at the time of the substitution, thanks to goals from Michael Owen and David Beckham. After the match the sports writers were quick to point out that young Rooney had been England's liveliest player, despite the fact he was only involved at the tail end of the game.

Wayne's brief but brilliant performance against Liechtenstein caused Sven to have a change of heart when England faced Turkey in Sunderland four days later. Despite earlier claiming that to put so young a lad into a game of such high intensity would be 'unfair', the coach now included him in the starting line-up at the Stadium of Light.

WAYNE ROONEY
WAYNE ROONEY
WAYNE ROONEY
WAYNE ROONEY

WAYNE'S HISTORIC ENGLAND DEBUT MATCH

Friendly International
Played on 12 February 2003, at Upton Park
ENGLAND 1, AUSTRALIA 3

ENGLAND

First Half line-up:
James, Neville G, Cole A, Lampard, Campbell, Ferdinand, Beckham, Scholes, Beattie, Owen, Dyer
Second Half line-up:
Robinson, Mills, Konchesky, Jenas, Brown, King, Murphy, Rooney, Jeffers, Vassell, Hargreaves
Scorer: **Jeffers 70**

AUSTRALIA

Schwarzer, Neill, Lazaridis, Okon, Popovic, Moore, Emerton, Skoko (Bresciano 46), Chipperfield (Grella 76), Viduka (Sterjoski 84), Kewell (Aloisi 56)
Scorers: **Popovic 17, Kewell 42, Emerton 84**

ENGLAND CALLING!

In the event Rooney repaid the boss's faith in him by putting in a truly inspirational performance as England battled against their toughest Group 7 opponents and emerged with a well-deserved 2-0 victory. After a relatively quiet start, the youngster was suddenly here, there and everywhere, creating a couple of chances for Michael Owen, and linking well with Owen's replacement Darius Vassell when the Liverpool-man hobbled off injured.

Vassell finally broke the deadlock on 75 minutes, putting England ahead when following up on a Rio Ferdinand volley that was parried into his path by Turkish goalkeeper Rustu. In the dying minutes Kieron Dyer replaced Wayne, and within seconds of the substitution a Turkish defender brought Dyer down. The resulting penalty was duly converted by David Beckham, earning England a much-needed win and lifting them to the top of the table.

After the game young Rooney was named Man of the Match and some pundits were already tipping him to be the man to inspire England to lift the European Championship in 2004.

Wayne's next England appearance was in a friendly encounter with Serbia & Montenegro at Leicester City's Walkers Stadium on 3 June 2003. This time he substituted for Michael Owen in the 46th minute when the scoreline stood at 1-1. England's opener had come from Steven Gerrard; Joe Cole, another sub, assured a Three Lions' victory with a stunning free-kick on 83 minutes.

Next up was the all-important qualifier against Slovakia at Middlesbrough's Riverside Stadium on 11 June. This time Wayne started the game, but was paid extra special attention by the Slovakian defence which effectively shackled him the first half in which the visitors took the lead through Vladimir Janocko. On 58 minutes Darius Vassell replaced the out-of-sorts Rooney.

Regular skipper David Beckham was under suspension at the time, so Michael Owen wore the captain's armband. And it was Owen, in his 50th international appearance, who rescued the day for England with two excellent second-half goals, after missing several chances in the first period.

The 2-1 victory kept England on track for qualification for the 2004 finals in Portugal. And despite his substitution Wayne was looking forward to collecting his sixth cap and, hopefully, netting his first international goal – and he was still only 17...

SEE **WAYNE ROONEY** – EURO STAR ON PAGE 32

ENGLAND'S TOP 10
YOUNGEST DEBUTANTS

1. **WAYNE ROONEY (Everton)** v Australia on 12 February 2003, aged 17 years 111 days

2. **JAMES PRINSEP (Clapham Rovers)** v Scotland on 5 April 1879, aged 17 years 253 days

3. **THURSTON 'TOT' ROSTRON (Darwen)** v Wales on 26 February 1881, aged 17 years 312 days

4. **CLEMENT MITCHELL (Upton Park)** v Wales on 15 March 1880, aged 18 years 24 days

5. **MICHAEL OWEN (Liverpool)** v Chile on 11 February 1998, aged 18 years 59 days

6. **DUNCAN EDWARDS (Manchester United)** v Scotland on 2 April 1955, aged 18 years 184 days

7. **JIMMY BROWN (Blackburn Rovers)** v Wales on 26 February 1891, aged 18 years 211 days

8. **ARTHUR 'BOY' BROWN (Sheffield United)** v Wales on 29 February 1904, aged 18 years 330 days

9. **RIO FERDINAND (West Ham United)** v Cameroon on 15 November 1997, aged 19 years 8 days

10. **TOMMY LAWTON (Everton)** v Wales on 22 October 1938, aged 19 years 16 days

THE MOST WANTED MAN

Wayne Rooney's reputation continued to grow throughout the 2003-04 season. Indeed, his inescapable presence in both the club and international arenas quickly made him the most highly prized player in world football.

Meanwhile, David Moyes was keen to keep Everton's teenage protégé out of the limelight as much as possible. But the insatiable appetite of the sporting media would make that an almost impossible task. Even before the season was properly underway, Wayne found himself at the centre of an injury scare when Everton met Rangers in a pre-season friendly at Ibrox Park in Glasgow. The youngster was hurt in a tackle and was carried off to receive treatment for an ankle ligament injury.

Although not fully fit, Rooney returned to action as a sub for Tobias Linderoth in the second half of Everton's opening Premier League fixture of the season against Arsenal at Highbury.

It was an ill-tempered encounter that saw both sides reduced to ten men – and the result was a great disappointment for the Blues. They lost 2-1, putting a dent in the club's ambition to build on the momentum of their 7th-place finish in the previous season.

Around this time Wayne found himself at the centre of a 'club v country' controversy, with David Moyes advising England coach Sven-Goran Eriksson to leave the less-then-fit lad out of his plans for the upcoming friendly with Croatia at Portman Road, Ipswich. (This was the second time that Everton's manager had challenged Rooney's selection by the FA. In the previous season he had protested about the youngster's inclusion on England's friendly tour to South Africa.)

Seven days after losing to Arsenal another London side, Fulham, provided the opposition for Goodison Park's first game of the new season. This time Everton won 3-1 thanks largely to an inspired Rooney performance that saw him involved in the creation of all three of the Toffees' goals.

Wayne notched his own first goal of the season against Charlton at The Valley in south-east London on 26 August 2003. It was a stunning, point-saving late equaliser that took the score-line to 2-2 in Everton's third Premiership encounter of the campaign.

Next up was the season's first Merseyside derby, which Liverpool won by a convincing 3-0 margin in front of an utterly disappointed Goodison Park crowd who saw several chances go begging for the home side.

Seven days later Wayne's spirits were roused as he starred in England's vital European Championship qualifying victory over Macedonia. He even netted his first senior international goal in the game, which was played in the hostile atmosphere generated by the home fans in Skopke.

The strike, which brought England level with the Macedonians at 1-1, enhanced the Rooney Legend. At 17 years and 317 days he had just become England's youngest-ever goalscorer. That goal inspired England's comeback and they eventually rescued all three points when David Beckham scored from the penalty-spot in the 63rd minute.

England were in Euro qualifying action again on 10 September for the return Group 7 meeting with Liechtenstein. This match would mark Wayne's third appearance at Old Trafford, the home of Manchester United, and his first victory there. And he scored again, in the 52nd minute, at *almost* the same point on the clock as he had done against Macedonia. This time he netted England's second goal as they secured the points with a 2-0 win. *(There's more about Wayne's England career on pages 32-39.)*

THE STRIKE, WHICH BROUGHT ENGLAND LEVEL WITH THE MACEDONIANS AT 1–1, ENHANCED THE ROONEY LEGEND.

THE MOST WANTED MAN

While Rooney's personal star continued to rise in 2003-04, Everton's on-field fortunes were failing to match up to the club's lofty ambitions. After the relative success of the previous campaign, notable cracks were beginning to appear in their armour.

Ironically, part of the problem lay in manager Moyes' desire to shield Wayne Rooney from the pressures of the game while at the same time giving him a fair share of Premier League football. The starry youngster was consequently played in a variety of positions throughout the season and, while he accepted each task with all his inbuilt enthusiasm and energy, he did not enjoy a consistent role in the Everton set-up.

eight substitute appearances.

But, of course, any team that achieves a measure of success in the Premiership generally needs a striker (preferably two or more) to achieve double figures in the scoring stakes. Everton eventually suffered from their lack of goals at one end and a leaky defence at the other by finishing 17th, one rung above the drop zone which saw Leicester, Leeds and Wolves all saying farewell to top-flight football.

It was on the international front that Wayne had really forged ahead. Following his goals against Macedonia and Liechtenstein, he was next in the thick of things in England's vital Euro clash with Turkey in Istanbul where the hostile atmosphere

THE THREE LIONS HAD QUALIFIED FOR THE EUROPEAN CHAMPIONSHIP FINALS IN PORTUGAL AND WAYNE WOULD PLAY FOR ENGLAND IN FIVE MORE FRIENDLY GAMES BEFORE HIS GREAT EURO ADVENTURE BEGAN.

After his sensational strike against Charlton in August, he did not score again in the Premiership until almost half way through the season when Everton met Portsmouth at Fratton Park in early December. It was a cracking match-winning strike on 42 minutes that secured the Toffees' first away victory of the season.

After that Wayne bagged a further seven goals for the Toffees. There were singles at home to Leicester and Birmingham, two in a hard-fought 3-3 draw at Southampton, another against Pompey at Goodison Park, another at Leicester and finally the opener in a 1-1 draw with Leeds at Elland Road.

All this newsworthy net-bulging made him Everton's top scorer of 2003-04 with nine League goals in 26 Premier League starts and

was even more intense than that faced by England's players in Macedonia four months earlier. In the event, England produced a magnificent stonewall performance to emerge with the required point from a 0-0 draw.

The Three Lions had qualified for the European Championship Finals in Portugal and Wayne would play for England in five more friendly games before his great Euro adventure began.

Football's Most Wanted Man was in the news for other reasons too. Despite Everton's reluctance to part with their star player, it seemed that his transfer to a bigger club was looking inevitable. In the money-dominated world of football, the Merseyside Blues could hardly afford not to let him go when the offers rolled in...

WAYNE-WORDS

SEE HOW QUICKLY
YOU CAN FIND 20
WAYNE-WORDS
HIDDEN IN THE GRID.
THEY MAY READ UP,
DOWN, FORWARDS,
BACKWARDS OR
HORIZONTALLY.

- BECKHAM
- BLUE
- CORNER
- DEVILS
- ENGLAND
- ERIKSSON
- EVERTON
- GIGGS
- GOALS
- GOODISON
- FERGUSON
- MANCHESTER
- PENALTY
- RED
- RONALDO
- ROONEY
- TOFFEES
- TRAFFORD
- UNITED
- WAYNE

```
W A Y N E A E H K I E
R B E Z A Q V K L B R
S D N C U P E M G J I
V G O A L S R T O G K
E W O E T O T F O C S
N T R A F F O R D J S
G D E F G E N X I P O
L F I G U R Y X S H N
A B H L N G G Y O D E
N C B H I U I E N N K
D E V I L S X G J F M
Z W O M D O O Q G W P
L X U C A N R Y S S O
M A N C H E S T E R D
N B I T O J K L U L L
A P T V Z R L A S Y A
M N E O P Q N N D U N
T R D T O F F E E S O
B E C K H A M P R V R
```

30

SPOT THE DIFFERENCES

WAYNE ROONEY
WAYNE ROONEY
WAYNE ROONEY
WAYNE ROONEY

SEE IF YOU CAN FIND SIX DIFFERENCES BETWEEN THESE TWO PICTURES...

WAYNE ROONEY

Wayne had collected his sixth England cap against Macedonia in the European Championship Group 7 qualifying match in Skopje on 6 September 2003. And along with his squad-mates he endured the hostile atmosphere and general bad feeling aimed at the Three Lions squad by the fervent home fans.

Being thoroughly professional, there was no way that the English players were intimidated by the angry crowd – but Wayne was concerned about his relatively poor first half performance in the match. Sven-Goran Eriksson had been concerned about it too and, with his side a goal down at half-time, he altered his game-plan and instructed the lad to play the second period in an unfamiliar support role to the strikers.

The ploy worked, especially in the 53rd minute when an ever-alert Rooney latched onto a headed pass from Frank Lampard to net England's equaliser. It was his first senior international goal and the one that secured his place in the record books as his country's youngest senior goalscorer. Ten minutes later a David Beckham spot-kick sealed the result for the Three Lions.

England were in Euro qualifying action again on 10 September 2003 in the return Group 7

Sven weighs up his options

meeting with Liechtenstein. Once again Sven deployed him as support to the main strikers, and once again Rooney took the task in his stride – earning the Man of the Match plaudits into the bargain. His goal, on 52 minutes, was England's second. Michael Owen had netted the first just after half-time.

WAYNE'S EIGHTH CAP CAME IN THE MOST IMPORTANT MATCH OF HIS INTERNATIONAL CAREER SO FAR.

Rooney's eighth cap came in the most important match of his international career so far. To finish top of Group 7 and therefore avoid the dreaded Euro qualification play-offs, England required a single point from their last Group game, against Turkey in Istanbul on 11 October. The atmosphere there was even more intense than it had been when England had beaten Macedonia in Skopje a month earlier. Faced with the prospect of potential trouble the FA had declined its usual allocation of tickets for the game, which meant there would be no Three Lions fans present in the stadium to cheer England on.

Beckham lets rip!

But Sven's Men knew they were there to do a job and, no matter what obstacles were put in their way, nothing would distract them from the task in hand. Wayne played his part in the drama, and he played it to perfection. The team performed with exemplary discipline – and would probably have taken the three points on offer if David Beckham had not missed a spot-kick.

In the end it was a case of 'Job Done'. The 0-0 scoreline in Istanbul was greeted by English fans with the same level of delight as the famous 5-1 defeat of Germany in Munich in 2001 and the celebrated 1-0 win against Argentina at the 2002 World Cup finals in Japan.

England had finished top of the Group 7 table and would be off to Portugal the following summer.

WAYNE ROONEY
EURO STAR

Wayne was fully involved in Sven-Goran Eriksson's preparations for the 2004 European Championship finals. He played in all five friendlies before England's departure for Lisbon in June. Those fixtures presented Sven with further opportunities to hone his squad choices for the big tournament – and because of their experimental nature, Wayne found himself substituted in each of the games.

He scored England's opening goal in a 3-2 defeat by Denmark at Old Trafford in November 2003 and netted twice in the only English victory of the series, a 6-1 drubbing of Iceland at The City of Manchester Stadium on 5 June. The other home game, also at the home of Manchester City, was a 1-1 draw with Japan, while a visit to Faro in Portugal ended all-square at 1-1 and a trip to Gothenburg saw England defeated 1-0 by Sweden.

Even after all that had happened to him, it must have been difficult for Wayne Rooney to believe that he was actually on board the team coach carrying the England team to Lisbon's Estadio Da Luz on 13 June 2004. After all, he had made his senior debut as an Everton Rookie just 26 months earlier. Now he was an established and important member of the England squad travelling to the biggest match of his career to date.

That Sunday the route to the stadium was lined with England fans chanting, yelling, singing and waving their red-and-white Cross of St George flags. And the name they hollered loudest of all was 'Roo-ney! Roo-ney! Roo-ney!'

England were drawn in Group B along with Switzerland, Croatia and France. The first game, against France, was billed as the toughest of them all, as England's cross-channel neighbours were the reigning European champions.

Despite the fact that *Les Bleus* boasted some of the finest footballing talent around – Zidane, Henry, Barthez, Vieira, Trezeguet and Pires and all – England appeared to have their measure in Lisbon, especially when Chelsea star Frank Lampard headed the opening goal in the 38th minute. The team in white then battened-down-the-hatches and clung to the lead for the next 51 minutes.

They might have gone further ahead if David Beckham had scored from the penalty-spot after Mikael Silvestre fouled Wayne in the box on 72 minutes. To be fair to Becks, it was an exceptional save by Fabien Bartez that had prevented England from scoring again.

On 75 minutes, with the lead still intact, Sven removed Wayne and Paul Scholes from the action and replaced them with Emile Heskey and Owen Hargreaves to tighten up England's defences. But disaster struck in injury time, when the remarkable Zinedine Zidane beat David James with a superb free-kick to level the scores at 1-1.

Worse was to come in the remaining seconds with Zidane again providing the pain. A poor back-pass from Steven Gerrard left James floundering with Thierry Henry racing towards him. The 'keeper brought the forward down, the referee blew his whistle and Zidane duly converted the spot-kick. The points belonged to France and England now had a mountain to climb.

NOW HE WAS AN ESTABLISHED AND IMPORTANT MEMBER OF THE ENGLAND SQUAD TRAVELLING TO THE BIGGEST MATCH OF HIS CAREER TO DATE.

Wayne in action against France

WAYNE ROONEY

Wayne had acquitted himself particularly well against France and so found himself in the starting line-up for the vital clash with Switzerland in Coimbra on 17 June. It was a game that England simply had to win.

He was a lively and persistent presence right from the off. And on 23 minutes he wrote yet another entry in the annals of football history, by becoming the European Championship's youngest goalscorer – at the age of 18 years 237 days. His goal came from a header after Michael Owen had set him up with a brilliant chipped pass. Rooney celebrated the goal with a spontaneous acrobatic cartwheel and his team-mates celebrated by piling on top of him!

Switzerland put up a pretty good fight, frustrating England at every turn, as they sought an equaliser. But with half an hour left to play the Swiss were reduced to 10 men when defender Bernt Haas was sent off. England took control and Wayne netted his second goal of the championship in the 75th minute. His 20-yard shot flew into the net after cannoning off the post and the back of the 'keeper's head. Eight minutes later Steven Gerrard wrapped things up with England's third goal.

Kieron Dyer replaced Wayne just after the third goal went in. Everyone acknowledged that the lad had done a great day's work – and his Man of the Match performance had brought him to the attention of everyone in world football.

Wayne was delighted with his goals and with his latest record. 'It's always great to break a record,' he said. 'But it's the team that matters. It was a big day for us and we came through in the end.'

HIS SECOND GOAL ARRIVED ON 68 MINUTES VIA A DELIGHTFUL ONE-TWO WITH STRIKE PARTNER MICHAEL OWEN.

With France only managing a draw with Croatia, England were now in a much better position ahead of their final Group meeting with the Croats. That game was played in Lisbon on 21 June and again Wayne was in the starting line-up. This time he produced another virtuoso performance, netting two goals after creating England's first for Paul Scholes.

Croatia took the lead on five minutes through Nico Kovac. Scholes' equaliser came an agonising 35 minutes later after the ball had zinged around the Croatian penalty box before Rooney provided the Man U man with the opportunity to head home. Wayne's first came in the 45th minute after Scholes returned the compliment of setting him up for a 25-yard drive that beat 'keeper Tomislav Butina. His second arrived on 68 minutes via a delightful one-two with strike partner Michael Owen. Rooney was substituted by Darius Vassell late in the game, and once again he was named Man of the Match. His four-goal tally also made him the competition's leading scorer, although he had already lost his 'youngest Euro goalscorer' record. Switzerland's Johan Vonlanthen had snatched that honour with his strike in the other Group B match in which Switzerland lost 3-1 to Group winners, France.

England finished second in the table and progressed to the quarter-finals meeting with Group A winners and tournament hosts, Portugal. Unfortunately, Wayne lasted for less than 30 minutes of that game in Lisbon. At that point England were a goal ahead thanks to Michael Owen's brilliant third minute strike.

WAYNE ROONEY

EURO STAR

Wayne was playing his usual exuberant game when he collided with Portuguese defender Jorge Andrade. The Young Lion tried vainly to carry on, but it was obvious that he was in some pain and in the 27th minute he was replaced once again by Vassell. An X-Ray later revealed that Wayne had fractured a bone in his right foot and was likely to be out of action for up to eight weeks.

England certainly missed him as the remainder of the match played out. Helder Postiga headed Portugal's equaliser in the 83rd minute and the game went into extra-time. After 120 minutes of full-blooded Euro action the scores stood at 2-2 with Frank Lampard equalising after Rui Costa had put Portugal ahead.

In the end it all boiled down to England's least favourite scenario – a penalty shoot-out. After David Beckham uncharacteristically fired the first kick over

'I DON'T REMEMBER ANYONE MAKING SUCH AN IMPACT ON A TOURNAMENT SINCE PELE IN THE 1958 WORLD CUP IN SWEDEN.'

the bar, things went to plan until Rui Costa missed to level the scores at 2-2. The drama was in the sudden-death phase when Vassell's shot was saved by 'keeper Ricardo for 5-5. To rub salt into England's wounds, Ricardo himself then stepped up to take a turn and beat David James: Game Over.

Although every Englishman was thoroughly disappointed to be going home earlier than expected, Euro 2004 had been brilliant for Wayne Rooney. His four goals made him equal second top scorer in the tournament, along with Holland's Ruud Van Nistelrooy (the Czech Republic's Milan Baros headed the list with six goals). He was also named in the tournament's 23-man All-Star squad along with fellow Englishmen Frank Lampard, Ashley Cole and Sol Campbell.

Sven-Goran Eriksson summed it up nicely when he said: 'I don't remember anyone making such an impact on a tournament since Pelé in the 1958 World Cup in Sweden.'

ENGLAND IN THE 2004 EUROPEAN CHAMPIONSHIP

WAYNE ROONEY
WAYNE ROONEY
WAYNE ROONEY
WAYNE ROONEY

ENGLAND'S EURO 2004 SQUAD

David James, Gary Neville, Ashley Cole, Steven Gerrard, John Terry, Sol Campbell, David Beckham, Paul Scholes, Wayne Rooney, Michael Owen, Frank Lampard, Wayne Bridge, Paul Robinson, Phil Neville, Ledley King, Jamie Carragher, Nicky Butt, Owen Hargreaves, Joe Cole, Kieron Dyer, Emile Heskey, Ian Walker, Darius Vassell

QUALIFYING GROUP 7 RESULTS

12.10.2002 Slovakia 1, ENGLAND 2

16.10.2002 ENGLAND 2, Macedonia 2

29.03.2003 Liechtenstein 0, ENGLAND 2

02.04.2003 ENGLAND 2, Turkey 0

11.06.2003 ENGLAND 2, Slovakia 1

06.09.2003 Macedonia 1, ENGLAND 2

10.09.2003 ENGLAND 2, Liechtenstein 0

11.10.2003 Turkey 0, ENGLAND 0

GROUP 7 TABLE

	P	W	D	L	F	A	Pts
ENGLAND	8	6	2	0	14	5	20
Turkey	8	6	1	1	17	5	19
Slovakia	8	3	1	4	11	9	10
Macedonia	8	1	3	4	11	14	6
Liechtenstein	8	0	1	7	2	22	1

FINALS TOURNAMENT IN PORTUGAL GROUP B RESULTS

France 2, ENGLAND 1
ENGLAND 3, Switzerland 0
Croatia 2, ENGLAND 4

GROUP B TABLE

	P	W	D	L	F	A	GD	Pts
France	3	2	1	0	7	4	3	7
ENGLAND	3	2	0	1	8	4	4	6
Croatia	3	0	2	1	4	6	-2	6
Switzerland	3	0	1	2	1	6	-5	1

QUARTER - FINALS

Portugal 2, ENGLAND 2
(Portugal won 6-5 on penalties)

PORTUGAL WENT ON TO BEAT HOLLAND IN THE SEMI-FINAL. THEY THEN MET GREECE IN THE FINAL IN LISBON AND WERE CLEAR FAVOURITES TO WIN THE TITLE. AGAINST ALL EXPECTATIONS THE GLORIOUS GREEKS EMERGED TRIUMPHANT WITH A 1-0 VICTORY TO BE CROWNED KINGS OF EUROPE 2004.

THEY MADE THEIR MARK TOO

WAYNE ROONEY ISN'T THE FIRST YOUNG FOOTBALLER TO MAKE A HUGE IMPACT ON THE ENGLISH GAME. HERE ARE SOME EQUALLY PRECOCIOUS TALENTS WHO LIVED UP TO THEIR EARLY PROMISE AND BECAME TRULY GREAT PLAYERS...

TOMMY LAWTON

Arguably the finest header of a ball ever seen. Tommy Lawton was a prolific goalscorer as a schoolboy in his native Bolton. He first played for Burnley and scored a famous hat-trick on his debut, four days after turning 17. He joined Everton in March 1937 and went on to set the standard for all Toffees' forwards, scoring 65 goals in 87 League appearances. He went on to play for Chelsea, Notts County, Brentford and Arsenal. He won 23 caps for England, averaging almost a goal a game.

DUNCAN EDWARDS

Just like Wayne Rooney today, Duncan Edwards had football fans drooling in the 1950s. Just like Wayne, he was burly, bold and brilliant. He was the shining star of Manchester United's famous 'Busby Babes' – the squad of brilliant youngsters gathered together by the great manager Matt Busby. Sadly Big Duncan died in the aftermath of the Munich air crash that decimated Manchester United in February 1958. He had played just five seasons of first-class football and had two championship medals and 18 full England caps to his name.

BOBBY CHARLTON

England Schoolboy international Bobby Charlton had the pick of the clubs when he left school – he chose Matt Busby's Manchester United. After scoring twice on his League debut in a 4-2 win against Charlton Athletic in October 1956, he was recognised as one of the brightest prospects in the English game. That early promise was fulfilled with a string of successes in United's colours and a World Cup winners' medal in 1966. The Bobby Dazzler finished his career as England's leading marksman, with no less than 49 international goals to his credit. No one has yet matched his tally!

JIMMY GREAVES

Jimmy Greaves burst onto the soccer scene on 23 August 1957 in the colours of Chelsea. He notched a goal on his League debut against Spurs and went on to score 112 more for the Blues. Jimmy netted a post-war record of six hat-tricks in 1960-61. Snapped-up by Italian giants AC Milan, he hated his time in Serie A and soon returned to England to become a star striker with Spurs. But for injury he would probably have played in England's 1966 World Cup winning team. His England career consisted of an amazing 44 goals in 57 appearances. He later played for West Ham and later still became a well-known soccer pundit on TV.

ALAN BALL

Blackpool ace Alan Ball made his League debut at the age of 17. Three years later he was the youngest member of England's 1966 World Cup winning team – at 5' 6" he was also the smallest player on display at Wembley that day. A tough tackling, tenacious and talented midfielder, Ball moved on to Everton six weeks after the World Cup triumph, became club captain at Goodison Park and led the Toffees to the English title in 1970. He later played for Arsenal and Southampton and was capped a total 72 times by England.

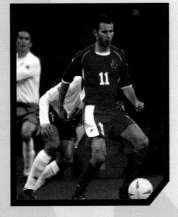

RYAN GIGGS

The Welsh international winger was born in Cardiff, but raised in Manchester. As a youngster Ryan almost joined Manchester City before Alex Ferguson stepped in to snap him up for United. Giggsy went on to become one of Old Trafford's finest servants and one of the most consistent British players of all time. So far he's won a whole host of honours with United and now skippers the Welsh international side.

WAYNE ROONEY
WAYNE ROONEY
WAYNE ROONEY
WAYNE ROONEY

PAUL GASCOIGNE

The precociously talented Gazza started out with his hometown team Newcastle United, making his debut as a sub against QPR at the tender age of 17. A few weeks later he captained the Magpies to their first-ever FA Youth Cup triumph, against Watford. He went on to become a Tyneside idol, before spreading his wings with Spurs and Lazio. His magnificent ball skills were always a delight to watch and his boisterous, fun-loving personality made Gascoigne the most famous player of his day. He played 57 times for England.

MICHAEL OWEN

Just a few seasons ago Michael Owen made a similar impact to Wayne Rooney – in the red of Liverpool. After eight Anfield seasons he made a big money move to Real Madrid where he now plays alongside the likes of David Beckham and Ronaldo. Michael made his full England debut against Chile in February 1998 and is now challenging the leaders in the Three Lions' all-time top scorers' list.

41

FROM BLUE TO RED

S till recovering from the injury picked up during the European Championship finals, Wayne did not play again for Everton. After his personal success in Portugal, a move from Goodison Park had looked ever more likely – and his transfer value had risen by several million pounds.

He could quite easily have become a Magpie, as Newcastle United began the bidding war for the youngster's services by making a £20 million offer to Everton. Manchester United quickly equalled that – and so the Tynesiders raised their bid to £23.5 million two days later.

Chelsea and Real Madrid were also said to be in the race for Rooney's signature. But it was Manchester United who finally settled the matter – in late August 2004, just before the 'transfer window' was due to slam shut for the rest of the year. Ironically, the deal was done on the day after Everton and Man United had met in a 0-0 draw in the Premiership at Old Trafford.

It was reported that the transfer saw United handing over the first £10 million of the massive fee to Everton, with a second £10 million due to change hands in August 2005. The Toffees were also due to receive around 25% of any transfer fee in the unlikely event of Rooney leaving Old Trafford. With other payments dependent on United's future successes, and on Wayne renewing his contract and making more England appearances, the eventual total involved could rise to an astonishing, till-rattling £30 million or more.

Whatever sums were actually involved, Wayne was now officially a Red Devil on a lucrative and highly envied long-term contract. He had notched an impressive tally of 15 goals in 67 Premier League games for Everton, now he hoped to improve on that with the Old Trafford outfit. 'I feel this can only improve my career, playing with top players in top competitions like the Champions League,' he said. 'And I can't wait to meet up with the team.'

Sir Alex Ferguson was just as happy: 'I am very excited,' said Old Trafford's supremo. 'I think we've got the best young player this country has seen in the past thirty years – everyone at Manchester United is delighted by this signing.'

Naturally those in Merseyside's Blue Zone were not so delighted. Although there was now a good deal of extra cash in the Toffees' bank account, Evertonians everywhere were devastated by the transfer news. The move had been on the cards for quite some time, of course, but still they just couldn't believe that Wayne was actually on his way. 'It was a tough decision to leave Everton,' he admitted when the deal was sealed. 'It's the club I've supported and played for all my life, but I'm excited to be joining a club as big as Manchester United.'

Amid much hype and hoopla at Old Trafford he was presented with the squad number '8'...

CHELSEA AND REAL MADRID WERE ALSO SAID TO BE IN THE RACE FOR ROONEY'S SIGNATURE.

RED DEVIL
ROONEY

WAYNE ROONEY
Nº 8

Wayne eventually made a sensational debut with Manchester United on 29 September 2004 in the European Champions League. Ten minutes after Ryan Giggs had opened the scoring against Fenerbahce, Rooney latched on to Ruud Van Nistelrooy's superb pass to blast home a 25-yard drive that flew past 'keeper Rustu Recber. Eleven minutes later he scored again with a low drive. The Old Trafford crowd went wild with delight – but there was still more to come from their new star. In the 54th minute he delivered a perfect free-kick to complete a debut hat-trick. United went on to win 6-2.

At Old Trafford that weekend he had his first taste of Premier League action for United, in a tough encounter with Middlesbrough who thoroughly deserved their share of the points from a 1-1 draw.

On 9 October 2004 he played his third successive game at Old Trafford – this time for England in a World Cup qualifier against Wales. England won 2-0 with goals from Beckham and Lampard, but it was Rooney who ruled the roost. He was involved in everything and almost got his name on the score-sheet after a spectacular solo run. Four days later he turned on the magic again, in England's next World Cup qualifier against Azerbaijan in Baku. The Three Lions side took a 22nd minute lead through Michael Owen, held on to it – and remained top of the Group 6 table.

Wayne next appeared for United in two 0-0 draws, at Birmingham in the Premier League, and at Sparta Prague in the Champions League, almost netting twice in the Euro tie.

On 24 October 2004 – Wayne's 19th birthday – United needed to beat Arsenal at Old Trafford in order to stay in touch with the Premiership's leading pack. But the Gunners were enjoying a brilliant unbeaten streak, just as they had been two years earlier when he first encountered them in that memorable match at Goodison Park.

With 18 minutes to go, it looked as though Arsenal would extend their run. Then United won a penalty. The Gunners protested that there had been no contact between Wayne and Sol Campbell, but referee Mike Riley was adamant – and Ruud Van Nistelrooy stepped up to fire home.

In the 90th minute Wayne got the best birthday present a boy could wish for, when a fine build-up by Louis Saha and Alan Smith presented him with a gift-wrapped scoring opportunity. The youngster made no mistake in netting his first Premier League goal for United and taking the final score to 2-0!

Having reduced the gap at the top, United seemed to be back on track. Then they went to Portsmouth and lost 2-0. Wayne was in fine form and at one point set-up Cristiano Ronaldo with a scoring chance but the Portuguese star fired wide. Three days later Wayne was in Champions League action against Sparta Prague. Like everyone else at Old Trafford that evening he marvelled at Ruud Van Nistelrooy's magnificent performance in netting all four of United's goals in a superb 4-1 victory.

On 7 November Wayne had his first taste of Manchester derby action, as a 77th minute sub, in a 0-0 draw with City at Old Trafford. In his next appearance, in a Premier League encounter at Newcastle, he was the star of the show, his goals in the 7th and 90th minutes contributing to a 3-1 victory. It was a brilliant result that edged United closer to Chelsea, Arsenal and Everton, who were enjoying a particularly productive season.

Three days later another international call-up took him to Madrid and a 1-0 friendly defeat by Spain at the Bernabeu Stadium, where he was substituted just before half-time by club-mate Alan Smith. A 2-0 home win against Charlton and a 3-0 victory at West Brom kept United in touch in the Premiership race, while a 2-1 victory against French side Lyon buoyed their Champions League challenge.

ROONEY

WAYNE ROONEY Nº 8

When Southampton travelled to Old Trafford on 4 December Wayne netted his seventh goal of the season. It came from a brilliant Ryan Giggs through-ball and was United's second in a 3-0 win. Around that time an Italian newspaper poll dubbed him Europe's Best Under-21 player, ahead of such starlets as United's Ronaldo and Chelsea's Arjen Robben.

Wayne next played against Fulham in a 1-1 draw at Craven Cottage, followed by an exciting 5-2 win against Crystal Palace at Old Trafford just before Christmas. The margin might have been wider if he hadn't missed a penalty on what was generally considered an 'off-day' for Europe's finest youngster!

Rooney was involved in an altercation with Bolton defender Tal Ben Haim in United's 2-0 victory on Boxing Day. Two days later United beat Aston Villa by a single goal at Villa Park. That was Wayne's last appearance before serving a three-match ban following the FA's 'fast track' investigation into the Bolton incident.

He returned for United's meeting with Chelsea in the first-leg of the League Cup semi-final at Stamford Bridge, which resulted in a 0-0 draw. Then came a return to his home city for the Premiership clash with Liverpool at Anfield, a game that brought a very satisfying goal for Rooney – the only one of the game.

He next played in an FA Cup Third Round replay at Conference club Exeter who had performed brilliantly to hold United at Old Trafford during Wayne's ban. This time the Red Devils took command with Ronaldo scoring early on and Wayne adding the finishing touch with a late goal.

Back in the Premier League on 22 January 2005, United beat Villa 3-1 at Old Trafford. On the 26th Chelsea eliminated United from the League Cup, with a 2-1 scoreline in the semi-final second-leg.

Wayne next performed a two-goal starring role as the Red Devils knocked Middlesbrough out of the FA Cup with a 3-0 win in the Fourth Round at the Theatre of Dreams.

Then came the visit to Highbury on 1 February with both Arsenal and United attempting to keep pace with Premiership leaders Chelsea. It was a fantastic game, a splendid advertisement for English football and a real tonic for United – who won 4-2. Wayne followed that great performance with another, netting a goal in United's 2-0 home victory against Birmingham on 5 February.

Four days later he collected his 21st senior England cap in a 0-0 Friendly draw with Holland at Villa Park during Sven-Goran Eriksson's preparations for the resumption of the Three Lions World Cup challenge at the end of March. Wayne went on to play in both of the upcoming qualifiers, a superb 4-0 result against Northern Ireland at Old Trafford and a 2-0 victory over Azerbaijan at St James' Park. The six points kept England firmly on track for a place in the 2006 World Cup finals.

Meanwhile, he had added three more Premier League goals to his season's tally – one came in a 2-0 away win at Manchester City (he also claimed the second, but it was judged a City 'og'). The other two came in a fine performance against Portsmouth at Old Trafford, a 2-1 victory. He had also played in both legs of United's Champions League tie against AC Milan. The Italian side won both games by a single goal and United were eliminated from the competition.

As the season continued after that disappointment, it was looking more and more likely that the FA Cup offered United's best hope of silverware. On 19 February Wayne returned to Goodison Park for the first time as a player, in the Fifth Round. The Evertonians let him know what they thought of his 'defection' to Old Trafford, but he took it all in good part and applauded the fans as he left the pitch. United had won 2-0 with goals from Fortune and Ronaldo.

ROONEY

In the quarter-finals on 12 March United met Southampton at St Mary's Stadium. Wayne produced a Man of the Match performance as United towered over the Saints to win 4-0 with goals from Keane, Ronaldo and two from Scholes.

That led to a semi-final meeting with Newcastle at the Millennium Stadium in Cardiff on 17 April. Whoever won the game would face Arsenal in the final, as the Gunners had eliminated Blackburn in the first semi. In the event the Red Devils dominated the game to win 4-1 with two goals from Ruud Van Nistelrooy and one each from Paul Scholes and Ronaldo. Now Wayne and his team-mates really had something to look forward to.

Between the cup-ties United had kept up their Premiership momentum, by increasing their run of unbeaten League games to 21. The run, along with United's hopes of catching the leaders, was finally halted by relegation-threatened Norwich who won 2-0 at Carrow Road on 9 April.

On 20 April Wayne was back at Goodison Park again, for United's Premiership clash with Everton – settled by a single goal from his former team-mate Duncan Ferguson. After the game Wayne declared himself delighted by his old team's brilliant season and wished them well in their quest for a 2005-06 Champions League place.

A week after their FA Cup semi-final in Wales, the Red Devils and the Magpies met again in the Premier League at Old Trafford. The visitors took charge of the game with a Darren Ambrose goal on 27 minutes. Half an hour later Wayne was struggling with a dead leg, and Alex Ferguson was thinking about replacing him. Then the youngster latched onto a ball on the edge of Newcastle's area and lashed a volley of such power and precision that 'keeper Shay Given was given no chance as the ball flew into the top corner.

WAYNE ROONEY

No 8

ROONEY

It was an unbelievable goal – easily the Strike of the Season – and it galvanised United into positive action. They eventually took all three points thanks to Wes Brown's first ever Premier League goal. Next day Wayne was named the PFA's Young Player of the Year, sharing the podium with Player of the Year John Terry of Chelsea. Wayne celebrated his status as the country's top young player by scoring in United's 4-0 win at Charlton on the following Sunday. That was followed by the visit to Old Trafford of relegation strugglers West Brom on 7 May. The Baggies put in a sterling performance to emerge from the match with a 1-1 draw.

United's last home game of the season brought champions Chelsea to Old Trafford, where the team formed a guard of honour as the visitors ran out onto the pitch. The Blues then put in a classy display winning 3-1 and setting a new Premiership record of 94 points (they eventually finished with 95).

Wayne won the Man of the Match plaudits in United's last Premier League game of 2004-05 at Southampton. The home side needed a victory to ensure their top-flight survival and they went ahead via a John O'Shea 'og' in the 10th minute. But United were back in it when Darren Fletcher's header went in nine minutes later. On 63 minutes Ruud Van Nistelrooy sealed the Saints' fate by heading home an Alan Smith cross.

United finished the season in third place behind worthy champions Chelsea and runners-up Arsenal. This meant they qualified for the European Champions League Third Qualifying Round in 2005-06. Fourth-placed Everton also qualified at the same level.

Next up for Wayne and his team-mates was the Big One – the FA Cup final against Arsenal at the Millennium Stadium on 21 May. This game turned into the 'Roon-aldo Show' as United's brilliant young forwards ran Arsenal's defence ragged.

The dancing feet of Portuguese star Ronaldo bamboozled right-back Lauren whenever the two came into contention, while Rooney was a menace throughout the afternoon – hitting the upright, almost volleying home a spectacular shot and generally running the show whenever United moved forward. His performance won the Man of the Match plaudits but, despite the fact that United had been the superior team for 120 minutes, he still finished on the losing side.

For the first time ever the FA Cup final was decided with a penalty shoot-out – and the writing was on the wall for United when Jens Lehmann saved Paul Scholes' shot. Wayne netted his spot-kick with what BBC commentator John Motson described as 'the perfect penalty'. But it wasn't enough. Arsenal's five nominated kickers each performed to perfection and the Gunners took the Cup back home for the tenth time.

Wayne's first season as a Red Devil was a case of 'so near, yet so far'. There were no medals to show for all his hard work, but on a personal level he had been recognised by his fellow professionals as the finest youngster in the game and he had lived up to all expectations.

MANCHESTER UNITED'S
ROLL OF HONOUR

ENGLISH CHAMPIONS
(Premiership & Old First Division)
1907-08, 1910-11, 1951-52, 1955-56, 1956-57, 1964-65, 1966-67, 1992-93, 1993-94, 1995-96, 1996-97, 1998-99, 1999-2000, 2000-01, 2002-03 (15 times)

SECOND DIVISION CHAMPIONS (OLD)
1935-36, 1974-75 (twice)

FA CUP WINNERS
1909, 1948, 1963, 1977, 1983, 1985, 1990, 1994, 1996, 1999, 2004 (11 times)

LEAGUE CUP WINNERS
1992 (once)

EUROPEAN CUP WINNERS
1967-68, 1998-99 (twice)

EUROPEAN CUP-WINNERS' CUP WINNERS
1990-91 (once)

INTERCONTINENTAL CUP WINNERS
1999 (once)

SUPER CUP WINNERS
1991 (once)

THE THINGS THEY SAY ABOUT *WAYNE*

> **"** He's the best thing to walk the planet... **"**
> EVERTON OWNER BILL KENWRIGHT

> **"** I can't see any reason to leave him out – and if he goes on playing like that I won't leave him out... **"**
> ENGLAND MANAGER
> SVEN-GORAN ERIKSSON
> (he didn't!)

> **"** Wayne is only 17, but Sachin Tendulkar didn't become an Indian cricket legend because of his age... **"**
> GARY NEVILLE, MANCHESTER UNITED AND ENGLAND DEFENDER

> **"** He is the most complete young English footballer I have seen since I've been in the country. He has everything you want including a low centre of gravity, which reminds me a little of Paul Gascoigne. Michael Owen is said to be a complete striker, but Rooney is a complete player... **"**
> ARSENAL MANAGER
> ARSENE WENGER

52

" Just occasionally, maybe once in a generation if we're lucky, there arises a talent so pure, so all-encompassing in its scope, that even the most hard-bitten and cynical of gnarled professionals can be heard to gasp in pure wonder... "

FOOTBALL WRITER
IVAN PONTING

" He seems to have the lot as a player – and if he continues to improve he can become an all time great... "

FORMER ENGLAND SKIPPER
GARY LINEKER

" Wayne Rooney is phenomenal... "

FORMER ENGLAND ACE
PAUL GASCOIGNE

" He's going to get better – which is frightening... "

ENGLAND SKIPPER DAVID BECKHAM

" He is definitely one for the future... "

EVERTON MANAGER
DAVID MOYES

" He can win us the World Cup... "

GARY NEVILLE

" He's precious... "

BRAZILIAN WORLD CUP WINNER
PELE

" He's missing out all the stages from boys' football to the man's game... "

EVERTON DEFENDER
DAVID UNSWORTH

ROONEY QUIZ

HERE ARE 25 QUESTIONS TO TEST YOUR KNOWLEDGE OF THE BOY WONDER...

1   WHERE WAS WAYNE BORN?

2   AGAINST WHICH CLUB DID HE MAKE HIS PREMIER LEAGUE DEBUT?

3   AGAINST WHICH COUNTRY DID WAYNE MAKE HIS ENGLAND DEBUT?

4   WHO WAS WAYNE'S FIRST CLUB MANAGER?

5   HOW MANY TIMES HAVE EVERTON WON THE ENGLISH CHAMPIONSHIP?

6   HOW MANY TIMES HAVE MAN UNITED BEEN ENGLISH CHAMPIONS?

7   HOW MANY TIMES HAVE EVERTON WON THE FA CUP?

8   HOW MANY TIMES HAVE MAN UNITED WON THE FA CUP?

9   IN WHICH SEASON DID WAYNE COLLECT AN FA YOUTH CUP RUNNERS-UP MEDAL?

10 IN WHICH MONTH WAS WAYNE BORN?

11 WHAT IS WAYNE'S MIDDLE NAME?

12 AGAINST WHICH CLUB DID HE SCORE HIS FIRST GOAL FOR MANCHESTER UNITED?

13 AGAINST WHICH CLUB DID HE SCORE HIS FIRST LEAGUE GOAL?

14 WHICH CLUB DID WAYNE FOLLOW AS A BOY?

15 WHAT IS WAYNE'S MAN UNITED SQUAD NUMBER?

16 WHERE DID WAYNE GO TO SCHOOL?

17 WHICH SIDE KNOCKED ENGLAND OUT OF THE 2004 EUROPEAN CHAMPIONSHIP?

18 WHO DID MANCHESTER UNITED PLAY IN THE 2005 FA CUP FINAL?

19 AGAINST WHICH SIDE DID WAYNE SCORE HIS LAST GOAL FOR EVERTON?

20 WHEN DID WAYNE MOVE FROM GOODISON PARK TO OLD TRAFFORD?

21 WHAT IS WAYNE'S DAD'S NAME?

22 WHAT IS WAYNE'S MUM'S NAME?

23 AT WHICH STADIUM DID WAYNE MAKE HIS FULL INTERNATIONAL DEBUT?

24 WHAT ARE WAYNE'S BROTHERS' NAMES?

25 WHAT IS WAYNE'S STARSIGN?

Answers on page 61

WHO'S PLAYING WHO?

WHICH TEAM IS WAYNE REPRESENTING IN EACH OF THESE PICTURES – AND WHICH TEAM IS HE PLAYING AGAINST?

WAYNE'S GAMES

WAYNE ROONEY
WAYNE ROONEY
WAYNE ROONEY
WAYNE ROONEY

WAYNE ROONEY

WAYNE'S APPEARANCES SINCE HIS SENIOR DEBUT IN AUGUST 2002...

FOR EVERTON – 2002-03

Date	Competition	Opponents	Venue	Result	Rooney Goals
17.08.02	PL	Tottenham Hotspur	Goodison Park	D 2-2	-
24.08.02	PL	Sunderland	Staduim of Light	W 1-0	-
28.08.02	PL	Birmingham City	Goodison Park	D 1-1	-
31.08.02	PL	Manchester City	Maine Road	L 1-3	-
11.09.02	PL	Southampton	St Mary's	L 0-1	-
14.09.02	PL	Middlesbrough	Goodison Park	W 2-1	-
22.09.02	PL	Aston Villa	Villa Park	L 2-3	-
01.10.02	LC	Wrexham	Racecourse Ground	W 3-0	2
07.10.02	PL	Manchester United	Old Trafford	L 0-3	-
19.10.02	PL	Arsenal	Goodison Park	W 2-1	1
27.10.02	PL	West Ham United	Upton Park	W 1-0	-
03.11.02	PL	Leeds United	Elland Road	W 1-0	1
06.11.02	LC	Newcastle United	St James' Park	D 3-3	-
09.11.02	PL	Charlton Athletic	Goodison Park	W 1-0	-
17.11.02	PL	Blackburn Rovers	Ewood Park	W 1-0	-
23.1102	PL	West Bromwich Albion	Goodison Park	W 1-0	-
01.12.02	PL	Newcastle United	St James' Park	L 1-2	-
04.12.02	LC	Chelsea	Stamford Bridge	L 1-4	-
07.12.02	PL	Chelsea	Goodison Park	L 1-3	-
14.12.02	PL	Blackburn Rovers	Goodison Park	W 2-1	1
22.12.02	PL	Liverpool	Anfield	D 0-0	-
26.12.02	PL	Birmingham City	St Andrews	D 1-1	-
28.12.02	PL	Bolton Wanderers	Goodison Park	D 0-0	-
01.01.03	PL	Manchester City	Goodison Park	D 2-2	-
04.01.03	FAC	Shrewsbury	Gay Meadow	L 1-2	-
08.02.03	PL	Charlton Athletic	The Valley	L 1-2	-
22.02.03	PL	Southampton	Goodison Park	W 2-1	-
01.03.03	PL	Middlesbrough	Riverside Staduim	D 1-1	-
15.03.03	PL	West Ham United	Goodison Park	D 0-0	-
23.03.03	PL	Arsenal	Highbury	L 1-2	1
06.04.03	PL	Newcastle United	Goodison Park	W 2-1	1
12.04.03	PL	West Bromwich Albion	The Hawthorns	W 2-1	-
19.04.03	PL	Liverpool	Goodison Park	L 1-2	-
21.04.03	PL	Chelsea	Stamford Bridge	L 1-4	-
26.04.03	PL	Aston Villa	Goodison Park	W 2-1	1
03.05.03	PL	Fulham	Loftus Road	L 0-2	-
11.05.03	PL	Manchester United	Goodison Park	L 1-2	-

KEY: PL = PREMIER LEAGUE; LC = LEAGUE CUP; FAC = FA CUP

WAYNE'S GAMES

FOR EVERTON – 2003-04

Date	Competition	Opponents	Venue	Result	Rooney Goals
16.08.03	PL	Arsenal	Highbury	L 1-2	-
23.08.03	PL	Fulham	Goodison Park	W 3-1	-
26.08.03	PL	Charlton Athletic	The Valley	D 2-2	1
30.08.03	PL	Liverpool	Goodison Park	L 0-3	-
13.09.03	PL	Newcastle United	Goodison Park	D 2-2	-
21.09.03	PL	Middlesbrough	Riverside Stadium	L 0-1	-
24.09.03	LC	Stockport County	Goodison Park	W 3-0	-
28.09.03	PL	Leeds United	Goodison Park	W 4-0	-
04.10.03	PL	Tottenham Hotspur	White Hart Lane	L 0-3	-
25.10.03	PL	Aston Villa	Villa Park	D 0-0	-
29.10.03	LC	Charlton Athletic	Goodison Park	W 1-0	-
01.11.03	PL	Chelsea	Goodison Park	L 0-1	-
22.11.03	PL	Wolves	Goodison Park	W 2-0	-
29.11.03	PL	Bolton Wanderers	Reebok Stadium	L 0-2	-
03.12.03	LC	Middlesbrough	Riverside Stadium	D 0-0	-
07.12.03	PL	Manchester City	Goodison Park	D 0-0	-
13.12.03	PL	Portsmouth	Fratton Park	W 2-1	1
20.12.03	PL	Leicester City	Goodison Park	W 3-2	1
26.12.03	PL	Manchester United	Old Trafford	L 2-3	-
28.12.03	PL	Birmingham City	Goodison Park	W 1-0	1
03.01.04	FAC	Norwich City	Goodison Park	W 3-1	-
07.01.04	PL	Arsenal	Goodison Park	D 1-1	-
10.01.04	PL	Fulham	Loftus Road	L 1-2	-
17.01.04	PL	Charlton Athletic	Goodison Park	L 0-1	-
25.01.04	FAC	Fulham	Goodison Park	D 1-1	-
31.01.04	PL	Liverpool	Anfield	D 0-0	-
04.02.04	FAC	Fulham	Loftus Road	L 1-2	-
07.02.04	PL	Manchester United	Goodison Park	L 3-4	-
11.02.04	PL	Birmingham City	St Andrews	L 0-3	-
21.02.04	PL	Southampton	St Mary's	D 3-3	2
28.02.04	PL	Aston Villa	Goodison Park	W 2-0	-
13.03.04	PL	Portsmouth	Goodison Park	W 1-0	1
20.03.04	PL	Leicester City	Walkers Stadium	D 1-1	1
27.03.04	PL	Middlesbrough	Goodison Park	D 1-1	-
13.04.04	PL	Leeds United	Elland Road	D 1-1	1
17.04.04	PL	Chelsea	Stamford Bridge	D 0-0	-
24.04.04	PL	Blackburn Rovers	Goodison Park	L 0-1	-
01.05.04	PL	Wolves	Molineux	L 1-2	-
08.05.04	PL	Bolton Wanderers	Goodison Park	L 1-2	-
15.05.04	PL	Manchester City	City of Manchester	L 1-5	-

KEY: PL = PREMIER LEAGUE; LC = LEAGUE CUP; FAC = FA CUP

WAYNE ROONEY
WAYNE ROONEY
WAYNE ROONEY
WAYNE ROONEY

FOR MANCHESTER UNITED – 2004-05

Date	Competition	Opponents	Venue	Result	Rooney Goals
28.09.04	ECLQ	Fenerbahce	Old Trafford	W 6-2	3
03.10.04	PL	Middlesbrough	Old Trafford	D 1-1	-
16.10.04	PL	Birmingham City	St Andrews	D 0-0	-
19.10.04	ECL	Sparta Prague	Prague	D 0-0	-
24.10.04	PL	Arsenal	Old Trafford	W 2-0	1
30.10.04	PL	Portsmouth	Fratton Park	L 0-2	-
03.11.04	EC	Sparta Prague	Old Trafford	W 4-1	-
07.11.04	PL	Manchester City	Old Trafford	D 0-0	-
14.11.04	PL	Newcastle United	St James' Park	W 3-1	2
20.11.04	PL	Charlton Athletic	Old Trafford	W 2-0	-
23.11.04	ECL	Lyon	Old Trafford	W 2-1	-
27.11.04	PL	West Bromwich Albion	The Hawthorns	W 3-0	-
04.12.04	PL	Southampton	Old Trafford	W 3-0	1
13.12.04	PL	Fulham	Craven Cottage	D 1-1	-
18.12.04	PL	Crystal Palace	Old Trafford	W 5-2	-
26.12.04	PL	Bolton Wanderers	Old Trafford	W 2-0	-
28.12.04	PL	Aston Villa	Villa Park	W 1-0	-
12.01.05	LC	Chelsea	Stamford Bridge	D 0-0	-
15.01.05	PL	Liverpool	Anfield	W 1-0	1
19.01.05	FAC	Exeter City	St James' Park	W 2-0	1
22.01.05	PL	Aston Villa	Old Trafford	W 3-1	-
26.01.05	LC	Chelsea	Old Trafford	L 1-2	-
29.01.05	FAC	Middlesbrough	Old Trafford	W 3-0	2
01.02.05	PL	Arsenal	Highbury	W 4-2	-
05.02.05	PL	Birmingham City	Old Trafford	W 2-0	1
13.02.05	PL	Manchester City	City of Manchester	W 2-0	1
19.02.05	FAC	Everton	Goodison Park	W 2-0	-
23.02.05	ECL	AC Milan	Old Trafford	L 0-1	-
26.02.05	PL	Portsmouth	Old Trafford	W 2-1	2
05.03.05	PL	Crystal Palace	Selhurst Park	D 0-0	-
08.03.05	ECL	AC Milan	San Siro	L 0-1	-
12.03.05	FAC	Southampton	St Mary's	W 4-0	-
19.03-05	PL	Fulham	Old Trafford	W 1-0	-
02.04.05	PL	Blackburn Rovers	Old Trafford	D 0-0	-
09.04.05	PL	Norwich City	Carrow Road	L 0-2	-
17.04.05	FAC	Newcastle	St James' Park	W 4-1	-
20.04.05	PL	Everton	Goodison Park	L 0-1	-
24.04.05	PL	Newcastle	Old Trafford	W 2-1	1
01.05.05	PL	Charlton	The Valley	W 4-0	1
07.05.05	PL	West Bromwich Albion	Old Trafford	D 1-1	-
10.05.05	PL	Chelsea	Old Trafford	L 1-3	-
15.05.05	PL	Southampton	St Mary's	W 2-1	-
21.05.05	FAC	Arsenal	Millennium Stadium	D 0-0*	-

(*Arsenal won on penalties)

KEY: PL = PREMIER LEAGUE; LC = LEAGUE CUP;
FAC = FA CUP; ECL = EUROPEAN CHAMPIONS LEAGUE

WAYNE'S GAMES

FOR ENGLAND – 2003-05

Date	Competition	Opponents	Venue	Result	Rooney Goals
2002-03 SEASON					
12.02.03	FR	Australia	Upton Park	L 1-3	-
29.03.03	ECQ	Liechtenstein	Vaduz	W 2-0	-
02.04.03	ECQ	Turkey	Stadium of Light	W 2-0	-
03.06.03	FR	Serbia & Montenegro	Walkers Stadium	W 2-1	-
11.06.03	ECQ	Slovakia	Riverside Stadium	W 2-1	-
2003-04 SEASON					
06.09.03	ECQ	Macedonia	Skopje	W 2-1	1
10.09.03	ECQ	Liechtenstein	Old Trafford	W 2-0	1
11.10.03	ECQ	Turkey	Istanbul	D 0-0	-
16.11.03	FR	Denmark	Old Trafford	L 2-3	1
18.02.04	FR	Portugal	Faro	D 1-1	-
31.03.04	FR	Sweden	Gothenburg	L 0-1	-
01.06.04	FR	Japan	City of Manchester St	D 1-1	-
05.06.04	FR	Iceland	City of Manchester	W 6-1	2
13.06.04	EC	France	Lisbon	L 1-2	-
17.06.04	EC	Switzerland	Coimbra	W 3-0	2
21.06.04	EC	Croatia	Lisbon	W 4-2	2
24.06.04	EC	Portugal	Lisbon	D 2-2*	-
		(*Portugal won on penalties)			
2004-05 SEASON					
09.10.04	WCQ	Wales	Old Trafford	W 2-0	-
13.10.04	WCQ	Azerbaijan	Baku	W 1-0	-
17.11.04	FR	Spain	Bernabeu	W 1-0	-
09.02.05	FR	Holland	Villa Park	D 0-0	-
26.03.05	WCQ	Northern Ireland	Old Trafford	W 4-0	-
30.03.05	WCQ	Azerbaijan	St James' Park	W 2-0	-

KEY: FR = FRIENDLY; ECQ = EUROPEAN CHAMPIONSHIP QUALIFIER;
EC = EUROPEAN CHAMPIONSHIP FINALS; WCQ = WORLD CUP QUALIFIER

WAYNE ROONEY
WAYNE ROONEY
WAYNE ROONEY
WAYNE ROONEY

WAYNE-WORDS - page 30

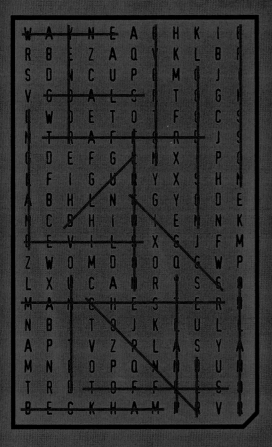

SPOT THE DIFFERENCES- page 31

WHO'S PLAYING WHO - page 56

1: ENGLAND & SPAIN

2: ENGLAND & FRANCE

3: EVERTON & TOTTENHAM

4: MANCHESTER UNITED & CHELSEA

QUIZ ANSWERS - page 54

1 Croxteth, Liverpool

2 Tottenham Hotspur

3 Australia

4 David Moyes

5 Nine

6 Fifteen

7 Five

8 Eleven

9 2001-02

10 October

11 Mark

12 Fenerbahce

13 Arsenal

14 Everton

15 Eight

16 Our Lady & St Swithins, and De La Salle Comprehensive

17 Portugal

18 Arsenal

19 Leeds United

20 August 2004

21 Wayne

22 Jeanette

23 Upton Park, home of West Ham United

24 Graham & John

25 Scorpio

WAYNE ROONEY

WAYNE ROONEY

WAYNE ROONEY

WAYNE ROONEY

WAYNE

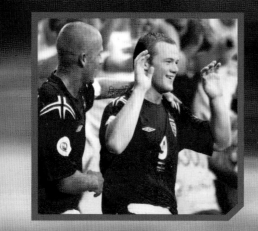